t'witterer
THE #WitAndWisdom OF
IAN McMILLAN

...in 280
characters or less

Published in Great Britain in 2018 by Dalesman
an imprint of
Country Publications Ltd
The Gatehouse, Skipton Castle, Skipton BD23 1AL
www.dalesman.co.uk
© Ian McMillan 2018
ISBN: 978-1-85568-373-0

Printed in China for Latitude Press Ltd.

TWEET T'WEET 'TWEET

When I was little, Mr White, my next-door neighbour on Barnsley Road, used to
fill notepads with what he called, as it said on the cover, SAYINGS AND APHORISMS
COLLECTED OR INVENTED BY L.WHITE, painstakingly transcribed from magazines or
books or made up from the brain that chugged away under the flat cap. At the time I
thought he was just eccentric but now I realise he was a proto-twitterer because what is
Twitter but SAYINGS AND APHORISMS COLLECTED OR INVENTED.

So I reckon Mr White would have enjoyed this collection of some of the many thousands
of tweets I've fired into the air over the last few years. I like Twitter because it makes me
think hard about language and how it works; it makes me write down my observations
and try and invent new jokes; and it helps me to float in an endless sea of puns.

Of course a tweet isn't as important as a novel or an opera, or maybe it is. Anything that
raises a smile or tickles a fancy or stimulates a brain cell is important, really important.
And next time you see me on a train or a street, do something eccentric and I'll tweet
about it!

Ian McMillan @IMcMillan

Twitter: Post-It notes on the fridge door of the mind.

Twitter: Wherever I lay my @, that's my home.

 56   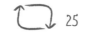 25   282

Ian McMillan @IMcMillan

I just open my mouth
and stuff tumbles out.

 3   8

Ian McMillan @IMcMillan

Me and my
dear old dad.

  10 264

Ian McMillan @IMcMillan

I'd rather be the cat's pyjamas than the dog's bollocks for purely aesthetic reasons.

I've got a hole in my sock. Still, that's preferable to the opposite.

 4   7

Ian McMillan

On the crossword compiler's 100th birthday he got an anagram from The Queen.

 45

 263

Ian McMillan @IMcMillan

You say Carmina
And I say Burana,
You say Burana
And I say Carmina,
Burana, Carmina
Carmina, Burana,
Let's Carl the whole thing Orff.

 1   11   28

Ian McMillan @IMcMillan

Night runs away
As slowly as it can
And day very slowly
Catches up with it.

     47   255

Ian McMillan @IMcMillan

A splendid day with first one grandchild, then all three. I sat there cross-legged like Papa McMillan, the white-haired fount of all wisdom.

 3   1   17

Ian McMillan @IMcMillan

Always the same early stroll for me, always trying to see new things. Sets my brain up for the day's thinking.

  14 184

Ian McMillan @IMcMillan

Early stroll. I'm a small boat blown around on the morning's open sea; I'm briefly joined by a plastic bottle that suddenly rushes away. Passing headlights smear my hunched shadow across a wall.

 10   64

Ian McMillan @IMcMillan

We pass a field where a black horse is staring at the ground as though trying to conjure up the rest of the chess set through thought power.

  19 178

Ian McMillan @IMcMillan

Schoolkids on the train:
"'Sticker over my nipples' is not alliteration!"

 4   8   53

Ian McMillan @IMcMillan

Two drunk blokes in suits on train laughing as they try to say the word 'inappropriate'.

Drunk bloke 1: "It's like Minnie Mouse and Mighty Mouse. I worry about you. You're lazy. You've watched the movie."
Drunk bloke 2: "Yeah."

  29 174

Ian McMillan @IMcMillan

Drunk bloke 2: "She is an enigma. Sarky comments."
Drunk bloke 1: "I never met her outside. She's franchised."
Drunk bloke 2: "She needs a chance."

 2   9

Ian McMillan @IMcMillan

Judge John Deed.

Did he? Ah dint know he were badly!

  38 148

Ian McMillan @IMcMillan

I always wanted to get my words on a tote bag. An ambition fulfilled.

You can't buy **BIG ISSUE NORTH** IN SHOPS, YOU BUY IT **on the street** FROM A PERSON **JUST LIKE YOU**
- Ian McMillan, Poet

 4   12

Ian McMillan @IMcMillan

Who was that little bloke you employed for the chicken census?

Oh, you mean The Brief Hen Counter.

  12 141

Ian McMillan @IMcMillan

Going to a football match on a Friday afternoon is like visiting Santa's Grotto in mid-July.

 16   9   108

Ian McMillan @IMcMillan

We're living through one of those eras when you wish history would take a gap year.

  20 140

Ian McMillan @IMcMillan

He used a squeegee board to contact dead window-cleaners.

 2   2   ♡ 27

Ian McMillan @IMcMillan

Nodded off on train; guard had to wake me up to check my ticket. The humiliation.

  32 140

Ian McMillan @IMcMillan

He was trapped bare-handed
In a gloveless marriage.

 2   2   ♡ 18

Ian McMillan @IMcMillan

50p piece stuck to the floor in Beadnell. Took me fifteen minutes to admit defeat.

 6   15   66

Ian McMillan @IMcMillan

Man on train: "Is this train going to Barnsley?"

Another man: "I don't care. I've just seen a donkey walk past."

Third man: "I would sack him."

  24 139

Ian McMillan @IMcMillan

The Second Amendment
In Northern Towns In Winter:
The Right To Bare Arms.

 6   15   66

Ian McMillan @IMcMillan

I've made my bucket list:

Bucket

Bucket

Bucket

Bucket

 6   15   66

Ian McMillan @IMcMillan

Happy Birthday to me! It snowed 62 years ago on this day when I was born, and I'd like to think, through a kind of weather cycle, that one or two of the same snowflakes are falling again.

 6   15   66

Ian McMillan @IMcMillan

Pensioner: "Get off your arse and do stuff, that's what I say."

Mate: "She has a drink problem. Makes herself wait till dinnertime, though."

 6   15    66

Ian McMillan @IMcMillan

They retrain bakers in the art of Japanese Theatre on a knead to Noh basis.

 6  15 ♡ 66

Ian McMillan @IMcMillan

This is my new performance piece: Middle-Aged Bloke In Dressing Gown Sups Tea, Loses Control Of Mug, Spills Tea Down Gown, Laughs Bitterly.

 6   15   66

Ian McMillan @IMcMillan

Sometimes I think my brain gets dressed in the dark.

 6   15   66

Ian McMillan @IMcMillan

At least they didn't put Dr Beeching in charge of poetry. He'd have got rid of lots of lines that didn't get read much.

 6 15 ♡ 66

Ian McMillan @IMcMillan

Baby Noah's coming. We'll go down to the library: I've got his card, the one that lets him access the world.

 6   15   66

Ian McMillan @IMcMillan

Captain W E Johns had to dig really deep to create his fictional characters: The Mined Biggles.

 6   15   ♥ 66

Ian McMillan @IMcMillan

I've got one of those books with all the place-names in.

Gazetteer!

Ask nicely and I might.

 6   15   66

Ian McMillan @IMcMillan

Time to revive that phrase my Uncle Charlie's son Little Charlie used to use if asked where something was: "Up my arse on the second shelf!"

 6   15   66

Ian McMillan @IMcMillan

It's the idea that people who use
apostrophes differently are lesser
human beings that amuse's me.

 6   15   66

Ian McMillan @IMcMillan

Self-appointed punctuation
pedant dies and arrives at the
Pearly Gate's.
Turns round and goes to He'll.

 6   158   263

Ian McMillan @IMcMillan

I love that bit in Snow White and The Magnificent Seven where Yul Brynner gathers the dwarves together for the first time at the gold mine.

 18   79   357

 **Ian McMillan** @IMcMillan

Edward Tubs

You are immortal

Until the tide turns.

 1   2   16

Ian McMillan @IMcMillan

IT is very important because without it Isaac Newton would just have discovered gravy.

 1   12

Ian McMillan @IMcMillan

Bloke in Penistone: "You wasted hafe an hour talkin' to Pat."
His wife: "You've got to be sociable."
Bloke: "Not wi' Pat."

 7   3   60

Ian McMillan @IMcMillan

RIP, Peter Sallis; you gave dignity to that bloke in the flat cap who wandered the Holmfirth hills and talked like all our granddads.

 7 2 39

Ian McMillan @IMcMillan

Early stroll. Morning's pale forehead on the horizon. A cat oozes by like dark paint spilled down a dark wall. In the shop, a man cleans a box of Maltesers with a feather duster.

 3　 5　 50

Ian McMillan @IMcMillan

Just stretched and accidentally wrote on the wall with a biro and momentarily though of blaming it on baby Noah. I'm a bad man.

 5   14

Ian McMillan @IMcMillan

I think I suit
a beret.

 3   4   72

Ian McMillan @IMcMillan

Saw somebody taking innuendoes door-to-door. He was from Deliverooermissis.

  2 11

Ian McMillan @IMcMillan

I love being a granddad, although sometimes I know I feel and look like that bloke on the Elderly People Crossing road signs.

 2   1   13

Ian McMillan @IMcMillan

I'm living the dream, which means I'm walking down the street naked except for a hat as turtles walk behind me playing recorders.

 3   13   61

Ian McMillan @IMcMillan

Alternative
Abbey Road
cover, Doncaster
Station.

 4   19   106

Ian McMillan @IMcMillan

"Nice to see you, to see you ...
well, you know the rest."
– Brusque Forsyth.

 4   17   ♡ 93

Ian McMillan @IMcMillan

Because I'm 61 I refer to it as my mobile phone and not my phone.

 2   3   18

Ian McMillan @IMcMillan

Ah, February. We meet again.
You look older than last year.
Mind you, so do I.

 3   3   21

Ian McMillan @IMcMillan

In the Bible, what was Ham's almost identical twin called?

Hamish.

 1 21 112

Ian McMillan @IMcMillan

It only takes a minute girl
To fall in love
With Tom Thumb.

 8 44 128

Ian McMillan @IMcMillan

Happy 150th birthday to the Shipping Forecast, mystical narrative poem of place and rhythmic air.

 3   2   14

Ian McMillan @IMcMillan

Let not shouty men
With bulging veins
Scream us into
More bloodstains.

 19 2 ♡ 45

Ian McMillan @IMcMillan

As he got older he began to speak Ancient Creak.

 4   3   36

Ian McMillan @IMcMillan

I liked that Oscar Wilde play about
the monster limpet:
The Shellfish Giant.

 2   1 21

Ian McMillan @IMcMillan

I'm going to manufacture a
perfume infused with the scent of
Yorkshire snickets and I'm going
to call it Ginnel No5.

 1 8 24

Ian McMillan @IMcMillan

Found poetry in
the gift shop.

 5   12   66

Ian McMillan @IMcMillan

Young woman on train: "I could do voices for cartoons. Mind you, they'd all sound like me."

Bloke in café: "Coconut milk? Is that even a thing?"

 6   17   79

Ian McMillan @IMcMillan

When asked in court about stealing seabirds the accused replied, "No cormorant".

 2   9   ♥ 31

Ian McMillan @IMcMillan

I've said it before
And I'll say it again:
Cold mushy peas
Eaten straight from the tin
Are a glimpse of perfection
That make this boy grin.

 3   2   26

Ian McMillan @IMcMillan

Where's the fake cathedral?
Kidderminster.

6   4   35

Ian McMillan @IMcMillan

A
Poem
Is
A
Ladder
That
You
Climb
Down

 5   15   56

Ian McMillan @IMcMillan

He kept his unwritten poems
In a bottle of ink.

 1   10

Ian McMillan @IMcMillan

My dad keeps signing up for evening classes.

Well, that's Pa for the course.

  1 10

Ian McMillan @IMcMillan

My mate's a lustful, drunken woodland god.

Satyr?

No, sat over there.

 1   11   37

Ian McMillan @IMcMillan

I'm going to record all the groans I make when I get out of a chair for a month and use them as a soundtrack for a dance piece about ageing.

 6   3   37

Ian McMillan @IMcMillan

Toilet pun, Huddersfield Station.

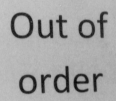

Out of order

We apologise for this inconvenience

 3   5   34

Ian McMillan @IMcMillan

Bloke on train: "I remember when the luggage fell on Dennis."

 3   9   ♡ 61

Ian McMillan @IMcMillan

If you're app-y and you know it
Tap your screen.

 3   3   17

Ian McMillan @IMcMillan

Splendid home-made Christmas card from young Sam!

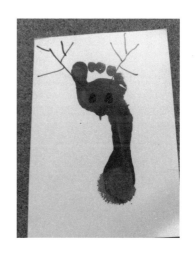

 3   3   21

Ian McMillan @IMcMillan

That 12-step programme was no good for beating my ladder addiction.

 3   15

Ian McMillan @IMcMillan

Bloke on train to his teenage daughter:

"Shall we go for a walk later?"

"A walk of what?"

"Of nothing. Just a walk."

"No."

 7 14 110

Ian McMillan @IMcMillan

Early stroll. I am held in a milkman's fresh headlights as rain plays intermittent music on my hat. A man in huge glasses wishes me good morning. A drunk tacks and staggers across the road like a boat on a windy lake.

 4   10   41

Ian McMillan @IMcMillan

For washing those big foam hands.

Refreshing
FOAM HAND WASH
ANTIBACTERIAL

 8   5   78

Ian McMillan @IMcMillan

The way the lights pass the train
And the train passes the lights
Like stars might interact
At the Galaxy's extreme edge.

 6   5   64

Ian McMillan @IMcMillan

His mind was a china shop that only employed bulls.

Took my horizon back to the shop; it wasn't broad enough.

 4   14   47

Ian McMillan @IMcMillan

My eyebrows are evolving into a Denis Healey tribute act. They seem to be in a different postcode to the rest of me.

 3   1   27

Ian McMillan @IMcMillan

This train seat's covered in salt and pepper!
There must have been a seasoned traveller in the carriage.

 20  55   237

Ian McMillan @IMcMillan

My granddaughter Isla looked
around the Darfield Museum shop
and I bought her a swanee whistle
so I'm in deep trouble.

 1   2   11

Ian McMillan @IMcMillan

The astronomer got a bang on the head
And for a moment he didn't see stars.

 2   2   18

Ian McMillan @IMcMillan

There should be
more men in pink
suits at stations.

 5   6   34

Ian McMillan @IMcMillan

Can't wait for Yorkshire Day, to listen to all the little squeaky sounds of the other counties moaning and complaining.

 4   15

Ian McMillan @IMcMillan

I walk downstairs like an Ian McMillan action figure in need of a new battery.

Afternoon's cosh biffs me to sleep on the settee.

 34    325   1.3K

Ian McMillan @IMcMillan

There appears to be mist round the bottom of your photographs.

Yes, I've got low selfie steam.

  110 378

Ian McMillan @IMcMillan

Early stroll. A dropped white bag like an exhausted ghost; the huge wooden gates are closed, inscrutable. The sky applies morning make-up.

  44 173

Ian McMillan @IMcMillan

I've got a zeitgeist in the house. It's like a poltergeist but it only chucks cutting-edge designer furniture around.

  21 82

Ian McMillan @IMcMillan

I wake up and stare at the illuminated face of the bedside clock like an explorer discovering a cave painting.

  1 17

Ian McMillan @IMcMillan

Do you want the fish and herbs yet?

No, there's a thyme and plaice for everything.

  26 140

Ian McMillan @IMcMillan

Overheard: "He had one eye going to the fish shop and the other eye coming back with the chips."

  8 74

Ian McMillan @IMcMillan

Can't wait to get home and stroll down to vote; that holy moment with the pencil, the string, the paper, the hopes, the dreams.

POLLING STATION

    5   52

Ian McMillan @IMcMillan

Off for an eye test; looking forward to reading that avant-garde poem they pin to the wall.

  3 44

Ian McMillan @IMcMillan

Take me to the bottom
Of your optician's chart
Let me try to read the letters
Written tiny on your heart.

  10 89

Ian McMillan @IMcMillan

Brasso, the Yorkshire Marx Brother.

Yorkshire pronunciation: The "It's my round" is silent.

  4 82

Ian McMillan @IMcMillan

"You, boy: help me with my crossword. 'Freshwater fish with teeth', four letters."
"Don't tell him, Pike."

  14 83

Ian McMillan @IMcMillan

Autumn has almost learned all its lines. It's almost ready to put the book down and walk on stage in the old costume of falling leaves.

  13 78

Ian McMillan @IMcMillan

The tide is like a teenager.

Comes in, goes out,

Comes in, goes out.

Sometimes waves in passing.

Ian McMillan @IMcMillan

Everybody has their own way of tiling a bathroom.
Chacun a son grout.

 4   34

Ian McMillan @IMcMillan

Crust
Almighty!

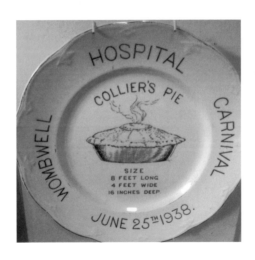

  1 31

Ian McMillan @IMcMillan

Note to self: stop writing notes to self.

I dropped my phone in the bath and now it's wringing.

  2 26

Ian McMillan @IMcMillan

Llandudno; memories of happy days with the kids at the Tan-Y-Marian. Sail that tiny yacht of past time on the boating lake!

  2 23

Ian McMillan @IMcMillan

Oh life, where have you been? Cleethorpes.

  3 18

Ian McMillan @IMcMillan

When you go to Jurys Inn hotels they always ask you what kind of cover you want:
Quilty or Not Quilty.

  1 16

Ian McMillan @IMcMillan

Are these real amphibians?
No, we have a problem with fake
newts.

  3 14

Ian McMillan @IMcMillan

The two arguing Yorkshiremen didn't see Aye to Aye.

Two jogging Yorkshiremen pass each other in opposite directions: Rapid 'Aye' Movement.

  14 105

Ian McMillan @IMcMillan

Discussing washing machine design with my wife. She says "If you designed washing machines we'd be all right" with just a hint of sarcasm. A hint.

  16 100

Ian McMillan @IMcMillan

Stroll image: good
to see the old craft
of tying empty crisp
bags in knots survives.

  11 79

Ian McMillan @IMcMillan

I hope that asteroid wins the Miss World title.

If you fail the chair-making exam you can resit it.

         18   63

Ian McMillan @IMcMillan

The clocks go back tonight.
Good riddance: coming over here,
taking our time.

  8 71

Ian McMillan @IMcMillan

The Barnsley equivalent of Spartacus:

> I was in Kes
> No, I was in Kes
> No, I was in Kes
> No, I was in Kes

  6 57

Ian McMillan @IMcMillan

Looking forward to a Cleethorpes day today:
The sun, the sand, the sea, the sky
And my mother-in-law's meat and tatie pie.

  9 53

Ian McMillan @IMcMillan

Early stroll. I walk under dancing shadows of leaves as the Moon's chipped snooker ball rolls slowly towards morning's blushing pocket.

  4 51

Ian McMillan @IMcMillan

@adelegeras: "Three people who look better older than younger: Theresa May, Mary Berry and Ian McMillan."

That's a fact. As a baby I looked like a tin of condensed soup.

  9 45

Ian McMillan @IMcMillan

Woman on Sheffield Station to her mate: "She thinks we're lower than pond life. Well, to be fair, sometimes we are."

  8 46

Ian McMillan @IMcMillan

Many cowboy films being made these days?
No, it's all quiet on the western front.

  10 41

Ian McMillan @IMcMillan

Yesterday meets Today on time's street corner and they agree to go their separate ways forever. Tomorrow is watching from an upstairs room.

  3 33

Ian McMillan @IMcMillan

You can sometimes detect
The early drafts of poems
Behind the finished lines
Like phantom pains
From severed limbs.

  1 21

Ian McMillan @IMcMillan

At the right end of the cue at the chip shop.

PLEASE CUE
THIS SIDE

  3 19

Ian McMillan @IMcMillan

As I write, a phrase swims by. I try to catch it and put it in the keepnet but it evades my bait and disappears.

  3 17

Ian McMillan @IMcMillan

Sometimes the alphabet is not
enough
For all the meanings and emotions
we need.

  0 20

Ian McMillan @IMcMillan

Happy New Year when it comes; let's be kind to each other and reach out to the ones who need our help.

    0   18

Ian McMillan @IMcMillan

Oh well, whatever happens later, I'll still believe in creativity and love and hope. And poetry, always poetry.

  3 13